Table of Contents

1. Introduction
2. Do not change yourself
3. Change your feelings
4. The first acquaintance
5. Communicate with others
6. Be an attractive personality
7. Take care of others
8. The good word is medicine
9. Start with common ideas
10. Do not be bad-tempered
11. Enjoy the sophistication
12. Do not gain enemies

13. Happiest others to become happy

14. Models of humans and how to deal with them:
    i. Friendly personality
    ii. The hesitant character
    iii. Coarse character
    iv. Slow personality
    v. The opposing character
    vi. Aggressive personality
    vii. The character that claims knowledge
    viii. Talkative personality
    ix. Friendly personality
    x. Stubborn character
    xi. Transcendent Personality

     xii. The person who is looking for mistakes

     xiii. Complaining personality

     xiv. Required personality

15.   Physiognomy
16.   How to politely criticize
17.   Social person
18.   Some advice on cute behavior
19.   What should I do now ?

Introduction

Man is of course a social being, and the number of people living in isolation is almost zero. Since the art of dealing is the main way to success, it is very important to constantly develop the Kingdom of Skills, or review it from time to time.

I'm Clarke Robert, what I'll be doing is reviving these skills in a quick and training way. I do not say that everything that will come with this book is completely true, but you have to try for yourself, what you find, try it in a way that suits your composition and personality, and what you do not see fit, leave it aside.

Most of what comes next is the result of personal experiences in life in all aspects, at work, family, friends, and even emotional relationships.

You will never succeed until you develop the skill of dealing with others, you will not rise in your work, and you will only succeed in your relationships when you are successful in dealing first.

I can almost certainly confirm that psychologists have not yet agreed on a description of human behavior, but rather is a cumulative set of observation and experience.

Let's go to learn this magic that captures hearts.

Never change yourself

I advise you first not to change yourself or change your common sense, because this is not our goal in this book. Many people have not yet discovered themselves, but people think they have discovered it.

Fully believe that you are a good person in this world, and you should be proud of that and yourself. Do not try to imitate others, as there are no two very similar in this world.

What will change is some detail of skills and chemistry in handling. What will be changed are some small habits that you will not feel if you put it under a microscope, but its effect is fundamental to your results and relationships.

Even as I write, I feel fun. What about you?

Let's go a little deeper.

Change your behavior

Fine human thinking is based on overcoming the obstacles that prevent the development of personality, so the question remains, how does the personality and behavior change?

Take a few steps to quickly break down negative patterns:

- **The first step :**

Determine exactly how you feel. We all know that people are overburdened and some may feel a mixture of incomprehensible feelings, and we strongly believe that feelings are the engine of actions. All you have to do is determine the unhelpful feelings accurately in order to eliminate them, which keeps the true feelings and not the mixture of imaginary feelings.

- **The second step :**

To know and understand your true emotions and feelings, and to invest that feeling of understanding. It requires honesty with oneself and honesty with feelings. The idea that every feeling that you feel is a mistake may destroy your honest communication with yourself, as well as with others.

- **The third step :**

To deal with negative emotions themselves and replace them with positive ones to deal with others. You must discover the behavior caused by this emotion during dealing, for example, if you feel lonely, you should resort to love as an alternative feeling of loneliness.

- **The fourth step :**

Arm yourself with self-confidence and the ability to change. This is the result of several successful attempts to change certain feelings and behaviors.

- **Step Five:**

To ensure that you can address any negative feelings about others in the future permanently. Does it seem difficult? Just try, it will be very easy and it is a fun way to understand yourself and know your inner composition and its causes.

- **Sixth step:**

Make a change, and make sure that you change your behaviors into creative behaviors that bring you results such as love, money and success, instead of the bad inner feelings that lead you to not progress and engage in unproductive fake events. So, control your feelings instead of controlling you.

- **Step Seven:**

Simply repeat the above consistently.

The first

acquaintance is art

One of the most difficult situations is when we meet a new person, whether at work, in life, or on the street, because we do not know anything about this person.

But imagine yourself sitting in a train with another passenger next to you. You may sit and remain silent, or you may greet with a slight smile and then sit down. Do you find a difference between the two actions? At first glance it is not much, you are just a passenger who wants to go to his destination, but whoever examines the two situations, we find that they go beyond minor differences, to bring terrible differences with the results.

In the event of remaining silent, you will be wary of mixing with this person or asking for something, while in the second case, a dialogue may open that leads to a request to lower the level of air conditioning or allow more space to sit, and the situation may end at the end with the exchange of phone numbers and friendship.

The first impression is very important because it determines the course of the relationship. You draw the path. It is the most beautiful art ever.

I will not go into the skills of body languages, first acquaintance, and influence deeply here, but I always leave the impression at which side I am meeting. Be sophisticated, choose your words carefully, be polite, do not open topics for the first meeting, do not speak politics.

Make it attractive to meet your kingdom and politics quickly.

Communicate with others

As I mentioned previously, communication is a means of understanding between humans, and it goes beyond one language to include the way of thinking, convictions, social status and means of assessing things.

It also includes communicating through the body language and understanding its details. It also includes written communication, so I am writing this sentence from my balcony at home. I am contacting you, yes or yes?

Do not be a person who just wants to live, work, pay bills, and then die. You have to make sense of your life, and it is more beautiful than being successful in communicating skillfully to increase your knowledge and take pride in knowing successful people in life.

To know that one of the most beautiful skills in communication is the skill of listening and listening to others. Are you interested in a person and want to strengthen your relationship with him? Just listen and listen, it's magic.

One of the most beautiful skills is tact skills. I can almost assure that half of those in positions in this world are distinguished in this capacity, be tactful and sweep the world.

Do you read what is going on in the mind of his argument to know what to say? Try to remember a situation of misunderstanding between you and a person and imagine that if you listened, understood, and behaved in another way, what the result would be.

Let's go in more depth to increase our understanding of the topic.

Be an attractive personality

We always feel that there are attractive personalities and we do not know what the reason is, and we always want to possess this character and of course there are ingredients for that:

The most important of these ingredients are the general appearance, because of the importance of being the entrance to the hearts.

I do not lead the appearance that we do not control who created it, but rather what we can preserve from personal hygiene and clipping of nails and a quiet fragrance. It is not necessary to wear expensive clothes, but there is a beautiful calm taste of clothes, which reflects the human personality.

Work clothes are different from travel clothes, they are different from shopping clothes, and remember that simplicity is elegant and elegance is beauty, be simple and elegant.

One of the most important ingredients is the smile. You do not have to be very serious, we are nice creatures and you should not laugh at a high level at all times. Balance is beautiful. It is impossible to see a frustrated and successful man, and if he is successful, trust that he is an instant success that will fail. Smile to steal hearts.

We will not forget the etiquette of talking and sitting. Be polite, do not mess with things that are not yours, until you are polite by looking at what does not concern you, be tactful and balanced, make your voice balanced level, compliment and not hypocritical, sit in proportion to the situation. Look at the kings and presidents how they sit, each site has a special interaction with this special about your sessions and your choice of words.

Help your heart. Listen to what someone talks to you, leave the best impression, stay away from bad traits, be generous, be simple, and repeat the simplicity of beauty.

Do not forget your friends. There are rights to friends, it is easy to get to know people, but maintaining this relationship is difficult. Do not interfere with what does not concern you and do not exceed your limits, do not be selfish, believe me, your friends will treat you the same way.

Take care of others

Do you know the thing that every person is keen on and it is forbidden to approach him with blame or blame? It is self-love. That is the thing that pushes people to do irrational actions, and it is the same thing that pushes them to act in a noble manner that does not lack gallant spirit. It is not difficult, whether we call this thing dignity, humanity, personality or any other name. It exists within every person and requires respect. Every person is unique and has a unique personality.

In order to maintain this value when dealing with people, you must be well aware of a number of facts:

The first fact:

We are all self-loving and this does not mean selfishness. Were it not for our love of people, we would not love ourselves, for selfishness is the result that a person makes love for himself a goal and no one else loves it, while normal people love people and respect others.

The second fact:

It is that the priority of any person's concern for himself is more than his concern for anything else.

The third fact:

Every person who deals with you first wants to feel that it is important to you, and that it represents something of value.

The fourth fact:

Every person who deals with you desires a real desire to feel that he is acceptable to you, because the person's sense that he is acceptable makes him acceptable to himself internally.

Fifth Fact:

The self feels hungry as the body feels. If the medicine for the body is food, then self-food is respect and acceptance.

Whatever you deepen in understanding the foregoing, you

will have the most powerful weapon to deal with people, and have the confidence to lead and influence them.

The good word is medicine

The good word has a great impact on people, and the best proof of that is what politicians use to direct entire nations through beautiful and polite speech. Beautiful words not only create feelings, but reactions. There is an old saying that says, "The kind word takes the snake out of the hole."

Use deep, not flat, expressive words. And you should not confuse simplicity with superficiality. Experiment with the effect of beautiful speech with people, you will see that it magically changes your condition and that of your interactions.

You may not be able to do this directly, but it should be done gradually. Take 5 words that you use frequently and write them on a sheet of paper so that you feel that it has a negative impact on people, and replace it with positive words or phrases, and watch yourself after several days you will feel better, and feel that what he used to say negatively has become used to saying beautiful words and this has become a characteristic of your personality.

This method should be used not only at work or friends, but also with the family and everyone you encounter in your life. If you don't take this seriously, I will tell you a secret: this training is an introduction to your emotional, family, financial and career success. Look at celebrities and successful people, and you decide.

Start with common ideas

People are similar with some ideas and convictions and differ with other ideas. When you talk to one of them, whether it is a first meeting or not, always start with the agreed upon ideas. This will bring these ideas closer, never start with different ideas.

When speaking of similar thoughts with a person, you subconsciously push him to say "yes" several times, and this is how he feels comfortable and accepting your different ideas at a later time, but you can imagine when you start with different ideas what happens. The other party will feel that you are completely opposite and will start speaking "no" without feeling.

He made a half-million-dollar deal in this way only. Anyone who feels shared chemistry will give you all the feelings and cooperation he has, even in the field of sales. The choice of shared ideas is taught in sales cycles as he studies anything else. What do you expect if I start talking to my client with different ideas? Simply, I would have lost the half-million-dollar deal. Measure all relationships between friends, family and work. Always start with common ideas. You will get what you want.

Try to remember a group of situations in which you only heard a word more than once. Examine this situation and remember the ideas that were discussed, and imagine yourself if you choose other ideas, what will be the result of your relationship with this person, and only apply that soon.

Do not be bad-tempered

Bad manners is a psychological deviation caused by introverting oneself, and this problem may be exacerbated, causing severe embarrassments for those who deal with it, which makes it vulnerable to psychological, physical and emotional crises. Believe me, if you were bad-minded, you would not be in isolation from the reactions to these problems, whether directly or not.

As we know, the body gets sick from time to time and must be pursued and treated, as well as the soul and morals, because it is sick to appear symptoms of its disease in bad manners, hostility and lack of respect. Hence, you must constantly monitor yourself to give her medication and treatment, and this will not be done through monitoring yourself and your relationships.

One of the most common causes of bad manners is weakness, weakness, worries, and even poverty, because of the effects they have of making a person less patient and less tolerant, and making a person's feelings delicate calves.

But do not let this evil horse fly if you suffer from some of the foregoing because it will add you further, but rather mention the disadvantages of this bad manners and its consequences and its impact on the one you love.

Did you know that the result of curbing this bad manners is beautiful relationships, love and money? Yes, we are talking about results and one of the most wonderful of these results is to get rid of this bad creation is the love of people. This is the great love that you may end up leading to. .

Enjoy fine behavior

Every society has its own customs and traditions, and what is good for a society may not be acceptable to another. But scientists all agreed that the sophistication of dealing is nothing but simulation and imitation of developed societies, and the behavior may become sophisticated when it develops into behavior without cost and turns into a habit.

These behaviors are not restricted to anyone, so any person can acquire these behaviors to turn into an actual practice while dealing with others. The definition of these behaviors is that these behaviors that lead to respect and appreciation for others, and every person who does not respect himself cannot accept these high-level behaviors or deal with them.

For a person who violates these behaviors, we find people, especially those who respect themselves and others, move away from it and from dealing with it. On the contrary, we find those who are keen on dealing with telegrams that people love being close to it, dealing with it, and even imitating it.

Classy behavior is acquired through a personal sense of what a person acquires from concepts from the family and from personal experiences, but it is certain that refining the mind comes by constantly refining the soul and getting rid of bad habits.

It must be mentioned that the self-refining comes from patience with the circumstances of life and difficulties and concern for the love and affection of people, and you will not be able to overcome the effects of these difficulties unless you are sincere in that.

Do you hear the term civility? Yes, it is taking into account our duty towards others and towards things and how to perform them in a proper manner, and taking into account the act of actions in proportion to the prevailing fairness and traditions.

High-end human behaviors are not limited to some specific rules but rather to good behavior in sudden situations.

What we know from the rules of high-end deal is to appropriately raise the value of the human being. Make yourself like a magnet to learn both small and large in this field.

Try not to gain enemies

From intelligence all people gain. I am not saying making friends with all of them, but moving away from making enemies. You may win an enemy in a situation or in an occasion of disagreement or misunderstanding. Trust me, this person will be on the lookout as soon as possible because you program it without knowing to take a personal defense position.

The relationship of hostility between people may begin to speak. Don't say to anyone who talks with you, you're wrong, but tell him yes but. You may avoid contention and hostility by changing the chosen word, because if you oppose the ideas of the person in front of you, then you ignite a wick for self-defense and his thoughts, and the situation will end up with a difference and hostility.

Don't feel like you're trying to learn it, just do it smart and kindly by choosing your words. Try this a few times and analyze the situations you are going through. You will become a wizard after mastering these skills.

If someone criticizes you, tell him "Yes it seems I am wrong" and if not, then he will calm down and attack him, and then gradually begin to prove your point of view. You will be satisfied if you succeed in this, but what if you start defending yourself directly will make the situation worse.

Yes, it is one of the most beautiful skills magic and comes with training, and remember that it profit you money, passion and success.

Please others to become happy

Every person prefers to deal with a person who is cheerful, smiling, and who accepts speech. This is the nature of human beings.

People tend to be happy, optimistic and avoid pessimism.

If you have to be happy from the inside in order to make those around you happy, find us with your life and enjoy it. Do not link your happiness with narrow goals. But be happy because you are a human being, and you enjoy small successes.

Then convey happiness to those around you. One of the best reasons for happiness is to provide the service to people in need of this service. This gives you meaning to humanity and makes you very happy.

Tell the person who is opposite to you what he likes that will turn into a happy person directly. Choose a topic that he loves, for example, if he loves cars, talk to him about cars and their types, and if he lives a Mercedes car, praise this vehicle, its qualities and the quality of its manufacture, it will turn into a happy person and the joy will spread in his heart. Whoever knows, this person may be your direct manager and raise you as a result of positive feelings towards you.

Take care of others and their hobbies, care about what they feel, care about their joy and sadness and what they are going through with special circumstances, provide assistance if you can, whatever kind. My dear lady, only take care of him, his feelings and the circumstances he is going through in life, and share him with passion with what he feels, then believe me, you will steal his heart.

Try training as caring for someone you didn't care about before. Talk to him about the topics he loves and praise him for his ideas and suggest beautiful ideas for him, and study the results of that. Yes, he will love you and try to help you without feeling, and repeat this act with one of your family or one of your friends or co-workers.

Be a good leader and be the inexhaustible source of happiness for those around you and get the results.

Models of humans and how to deal with them

Many people fail to deal with others despite all attempts. I think the reason for this is the lack of understanding of human nature as it should, and to clarify what is meant further, we will take a selection of models and their characteristics and how to deal with them.

Rough personality

Characteristics of this type of human:

He was tough in his dealings, sometimes even harsh on himself.

He does not try to understand the feelings of others, because he does not trust them.

Much of the boycott of others to hardening his opinion.

Trying to make others feel a sense of its importance.

He has the ability to discuss with design on his point of view.

He sees himself as fine and that people are not okay.

How to deal with this person:

Control your temper and keep calm.

Try to listen to it well.

Make sure you are fully prepared to handle it.

Do not try to provoke him.

Try to use your information and ideas.

Be firm when submitting your point of view and not hesitate.

Use the "Yes, you are right, but" style.

Friendly personality

Characteristics of this type:

Quiet and relaxed nerves.

He trusts people and trusts himself.

He wants to hear compliments from others.

Good-hearted and acceptable to others.

Unorganized and does not have time value.

He has a feeling of security.

Avoid talking about work.

He takes care of himself and others.

Let's see how to deal with this type:

Meet him with respect and listen carefully.

Maintain the topic being discussed and not deviate from it.

Try to direct the conversation to the desired goal.

Act seriously when needed.

Try to make him understand the importance of time and dates.

Reluctant personality

Its characteristics:

Missing self-confidence

It shows signs of shame and anxiety

Most of his positions are hesitant.

He finds it difficult to make a decision.

It gets lost among the many alternatives.

Tends to rely on laws.

Many promises and do not care for time.

More details are always required.

He sees that people are fine and he is not fine.

Let's see how to deal with it:

You must try to cultivate confidence in yourself.

Help him make the decision.

Provide him with a lot of information.

Give him more confirmation.

His understanding that hesitation harms his owner.

His understanding is that a person respects his steadfastness in his decisions.

A person with a slow reaction

Attributes:

It is cool and difficult to understand.

It is characterized by listening and understanding information.

He is not terrified by protesting the ideas presented.

Evades answering questions.

Not emotional.

How to deal with it:

Listen to him well.

Ask open questions that require lengthy answers.

Use silence with him to force him to answer.

Be slow with him and do not be quick to decide.

Show him respect and friendliness.

Opposition personality

Attributes:

He does not care about others.

Negative in offering his views.

Traditional and does not like new ideas.

He does not like imagination.

Stubborn, Crucial, Objectionable.

Not inclined to take risks.

He abides by the laws, not a letter.

How to deal with it:

Get to know his point.

Support your views with evidence.

Not giving him a chance to boycott.

Be patient while dealing with it.

Use the "Yes, Right" method.

Aggressive personality

Attributes:

Aggressive loves problems

It can be provoked easily

Hold his opinion

He rejects the ideas of others

It uses a personal attack style

Frequent shouting to terrify others

How to deal with it:

Listen to him well.

keep calm.

Do not take his words that touches your personality.

Hold your point of view and defend it with argument and proof.

Return it to the main points of the topic.

Use logic and avoid emotion.

Smile and keep the fun.

Use the Yes method, however.

The character that claims knowledge

Attributes:

Others do not believe.

Transcendent and loves to control.

Stuck to his mind.

He talks about himself all the time.

Skeptic, suspicious of the motives of others.

He tries to teach you even with your specialty.

How we deal with it:

Accept his comments, and make your point.

keep calm .

Use some flattery and praise.

Choose the time to boycott.

Be realistic with him.

Do not think about revenge.

Use the Yes method, however.

Talkative personality

Attributes:

He talks a lot and talks about everything.

He thinks it is important.

He wants to transcend.

Speaks many topics at the same time.

Mistakes made.

Imaginative, to prove his point.

how to deal :

Interrupt him in the middle of his talk, and if he tries to continue, remind him that it is not the topic we are talking about.

Show him the importance of time.

Show him that you are uncomfortable with his topics, for example, by looking at your watch.

Shy personality

Attributes:

Missing confidence.

Easy to confuse.

Trying to hide behind others.

His behavior is generally failing.

How to deal with it:

Ask him to give his point.

Do not give him alternatives, just give him the solution.

Point him to a position of guaranteed success to increase his self-confidence.

Stubborn person

Its characteristics:

Ignore your point.

He rejects the facts.

Hard and hard.

He does not respect others.

How to deal with it:

Others participated to unify public opinion in front of it.

Ask him to compromise a bit so that you can reach an agreement.

Use the Yes method, however.

The transcendent person

Attributes:

He thinks that his place is wrong and unworthy of him.

Try to phishing the negatives of others.

Treat others with condescension.

How do we deal with it then?

Try to be precise and practical with it.

Don't ask him open questions, because he will use the long answer to fix things inside.

Use the Yes method, however.

The character of the error finder

Its characteristics:

He hunted mistakes carefully.

He always has a question to ask.

Navigates and searches for lapses.

Offensive and does not respect the feelings of people.

How to deal with it:

Do not lose control of your temper.

Do not open the floor for him to speak.

Hear it the part you want most.

Remind him about the limits of his relationship with you.

The complaining personality

Its characteristics :

Many complain.

Many stories tell you of dissatisfaction.

How to deal with it:

In short, listen to him well and understand his problems and discuss them, he will feel a sense of relief, as he only needs to talk about these problems.

Required personality

Its characteristics :

Difficult.

It requires constantly and frequently.

Embarrass you to provide him with a service.

How to deal with it:

Use the method of dodging, by telling him that you will think about his request and talk to him later about it. This will give you a space to be able to tell what you can tell, because you will not be able to fulfill his endless requests.

Learn physiognomy

We have known the most important and widespread human models. Please note that any person may have a mixture between two or more characters.

According to what we mentioned earlier, the first step is to know the types and characteristics of people, and then how to deal with this type or that, but to see the issue on the other hand, which is physiognomy, a science that makes you know this person of any kind because of the shape of his face and its details. I repeat once again, it is not necessary to be completely correct, but it is a science that is being studied.

So, what are the features of a person and what does physiognomy mean:

Those with big, warm eyes are affectionate, friendly, and attractive, and dealing with them is emotional, relaxed.

Those with narrow eyes: They are very practical and have deep feelings, and they must gain their confidence in order to express their feelings.

Those with sunken eyes: they look serious, do their homework perfectly, and have a good sense of humor.

People with regular eyes: characterized by vitality and stability, and their susceptibility to humor

Owners of wide face: tend to self-confidence and take responsibility, and you can talk to them on various topics without the need to use flattery.

People with a narrow face: they tend to lack self-confidence, and they need to use some compliments while dealing with them.

Owners of the oval face: most of them have a calm ethics, meaning for life, characterized by the purity of intent and love, and usually this causes them to disappoint

Long face owners: they are serious and love life, and for whom deception and cunning may seem one of their characteristics.

The owners of the square face: they are characterized by courage and tend to be frank, bold and steadfast opinion, some of them possess vanity and self-love.

Owners of the round face: they are calm with their personality, and do not judge things except after careful examination.

People with coarse hair: they are usually with impersonal characters, and they need some flattery, and may suggest some suggestions while talking to them, such as loud voice and hand movements, and tend to walk outside.

Soft-haired people: most of them are as gentle as children, looking at life with an emotional outlook

With straight eyebrows: They love beauty and travel are self-confident, and they should be encouraged to express their feelings.

Curved high eyebrow: They are distinguished by the ability to express what is on their minds, whether with sound or with facial expressions.

After we know that a person's features may indicate his character and characteristics, you should avoid many troubles while dealing with people, by identifying what kind of person he is, and believe me it is fun and comes with training.

How to criticize without politely

Always remember that the goal of criticism is not to conquer the other party and crush it towards the ground and embarrass it, but rather to improve the behavior of man in a better way, if you want to criticize a person (and let your friend be) do not criticize him in front of other people because he will take a position of self-defense directly because of his shyness and embarrassment , Take it aside and express what you want gently.

And always remember that criticism should be for one time only and not by repetition. If you do that, you will be hunting for the mistakes of others and not advising. Do not resort to criticism if the topic is necessary. Use the utmost kindness, literature and smile.

Be skilled with indirect criticism. For example, follow the rule Indirectly indicate what you want.

Who is the social person

You know well that the first thing that people know about you about your meeting is your intelligence and then the sharpness of its nature, and after a long treatment, it is discovered if you are good or evil, but how can we be witty and have a distinctive effect? How do we have a strong social presence?

Is it heredity or factors that we gain from experience and practice?

Here are some tips, take from them what corresponds to your personality, and remember that making is a hated habit that no one likes, so if you feel that you feel difficult to be accepted, try to analyze your personality and the situations you are exposed to and your reactions and your opinion without being intolerant and without oppressing yourself, and remember that respecting others is The first step to accepting and respecting you, and I assume that you are a normal person with these tips. Without a doubt, if you are a prince or a famous actor, these concepts may differ slightly. Just take from them what you find that improves your personality and increases your social impact.

Try not to be:

Shy of the session: He is the person with few words, especially the new one in the session. Your main motivation must be your self-confidence. Try to remember the names of your addresses. This breaks the presence, and try not to interfere with the part that you know.

The hypocrite: He is the person who wants to win all the parties, even if that was through false courtesy. Sometimes saying "No" at the right moment raises admiration

Criticism of the session: It is the person who criticizes for or without reason just for the purpose of showing himself, not to say that you agree to everything that you hear, but do not criticize except when necessary and follow the rules of criticism that we mentioned earlier

Session star: He is the person who wants to keep the conversation within the topics that he knows and is good at. It must be known that people differ in knowledge and topics and any idea that you do not know about is also welcome.

The comic of the session: He is the one who tells jokes all the time, on the occasion or not, because the many jokes lose you respect among people, so be moderate in this aspect, and do not say that you are never frowned, because the sense of humor is the most beautiful thing, but beware that it is inherent at all times. .

Some advice on cute behavior

Try to realize the reality of the situation you are in, joy, sadness or a specific topic. Always smile and see the person talking to you (visual communication is aware of itself).

Speak in a clear, clear, high, and low voice (if you suffer from some embarrassment due to poor speech muscles, use some training advice for vocal chords and we will talk about them in another book).

Listen to others when talking.

Show blood wit only if position allows while speaking.

Thank the speaker if he informs you about new information.

Use the speaker's name while addressing him (it reinforces the idea that you remember, appreciate and respect his name).

You should be optimistic while talking, people are smart and can read your optimism and pessimism.

So, what do I do now?

You should train and then train, apply all the information mentioned in this book in your practical life and with all people, it will look like new at first glance, but you can imagine the fascinating results of this understanding and tactic.

The easiest way to apply what was mentioned, is to remember a situation that happened with you that simulates the examples presented and imagine if you behaved differently what would be the result. And start applying this thing with the first situation that passes with you. If you do not feel an improvement in the results, just go back and read the book again. I have deliberately proposed this book to be based on understanding and not on memorization, and I have deliberately been unconventional in my presentation so that I have summed up the conversation in the form of ideas, conclusions and results to achieve the desired and easy benefit

I wish you all the best

Clark Robert

www.ingramcontent.com/pod-product-compliance
Lightning Source LLC
Chambersburg PA
CBHW070256220526
45465CB00004B/1636